Red Kimono, Yellow Barn

Red Kimono, Yellow Barn

Poems by

David Hassler

Cloudbank Books

First Edition 2 3 4 5 6 7 8 9

Library of Congress Cataloging in Publication Data

David Hassler,
Red Kimono, Yellow Barn

ISBN: 0-9771973-0-1

Library of Congress Control Number: 2005935962

Cloudbank Books is an imprint of

Bedbug Press
P.O. Box 39
Brownsville, OR 97327
www.bedbugpress.com

Cover Illustration and Book Design: David Prittie

Author Photo: Gary Harwood

Production Consultation: Will Underwood

Cloudbank Books logo is a carving by Julie Hagan Bloch from *Haunting Us With His Love* by David Samuel Bloch.

Printed at Thomson-Shore, Inc., Dexter, Michigan

For Lynn and Ella

And in memory of Diana Cain Hassler (1938-1976)

Contents

I. SABISHI

II. THE PRAYER WHEEL

III. YELLOW BARN

I

Sabishi

Sabishi

I'm drinking coffee in the Shibuya
subway station underneath Hachiko Square,
named after the faithful dog, who,
as the story goes, waited here
every evening for his master.
The day his master died at work,
Hachiko waited until the last train,
and then came back every night
for years, to sit in front of the station.
I have seen his large granite paws
marking the spot for rendezvous.

Below him, I'm pressed against
the vent of a loud air-conditioner,
when two old women approach,
bent like cypress trees growing
in small trays. They watch me,
nodding and smiling to each other
and say, *Aah, sabishi des ne!*
I do not know their language well,
but I guess they ask if I am lonely.

I have left blue days in Ohio
to come here and be lonely, but
I cannot explain to these women why,
or what I think I have lost.
I cannot explain how I want to crawl
under the engine of my heart

and tighten nuts and bolts.
I cannot explain the mechanics of it,
why being lonely is work I want to do.
But I smile and reply yes, *Sabishi des,*
and hear doors slide open,
a soft recorded voice
announcing the station, *Shibuya.*

Reading on Trains

I do not know what they are reading.
The script falls down the page
like rain on windowpanes.
Heads bob as they read.
Hands turn the pages backwards
from last to first, as eyes
travel to the palm of the hand.

I want to let go of my language for awhile
to learn Kanji, "time."
The time it takes to learn anything:
The patience of standing shoulder
to shoulder in trains weaving
through the city, names of stations
slowing down and speeding up.
The time it takes to learn grass writing,
waiting for the moment when the sosho brush
with quick, barely legible strokes
touches paper — wet black ink revealing
the rhythm of our hearts.

O-bon

In sweltering August, on the last night
of o-bon, three day festival for the dead,
I arrive in the village of Komagome.
Families sit out at night on their front porches,
drinking tea or sake and tasting sweets,
wearing cotton robes they slip into
after bathing — bright, loose yukatas.
Doors left wide; orange paper lanterns
flicker to light the way, the dead
are invited to return to their homes,
tables set with their favorite foods
and flowers, instruments and books laid out
that they might want to use again.

On the first day the families went to meet
the souls of the dead at the water's edge,
and tonight they will accompany them back.
Everyone is gathered in a small park,
the ground neatly raked. Lanterns hang
from trees and around a small wooden stage,
where women in kimonos dance slowly in a circle
to the music of drum and flute.
Downtown, one summer, my mother and I danced
the polka on a bandstand at the corner
of Main and Water. We galloped
and spun as I held her hand, feeling the back
of the nylon dress she had sewn, white
with a little red and blue in it somewhere.
Here, the women lift their arms, appearing
only slightly from sleeves, where

plum blossoms and cranes drop softly away.
They turn their hands like fans and dance alone.

If I could I would find my mother's dress,
pick a bouquet of dandelions and place
the soft hearts of artichokes on clean,
shiny plates. I would put on the Mamas and the Papas
or Blood, Sweat, and Tears, leave by the back door,
the house bright and open behind me.
I would walk down to where the river bends
just beyond our yard,
meet her at the water's edge.

A Man Plays the Shakuhachi

He draws low hollow notes
from the wells of his lungs,
like the Priests of Empty Nothing
who played the bamboo flute
and begged in old Edo.
His tongue flutters a soft haunting
melody of rising wings and mist,
called "Tenderness of Cranes."
His fingers lift and fall,
as he bows over his flute.

Men have listened to this music of rivers,
growing old and taciturn, bitter in the throat
as the taste of green tea. Paper lanterns
float on wood, the names of the dead
brushed on their sides.

Eating Soba

I speak your language when I eat—
the silence of steam and scent
rising to me; red pepper, ginger, and soy.
This bowl's heat in my hands.
I snap apart chopsticks,
break the yoke of the raw egg
they call Full Moon that drifts
in the center as though in a pond.
I pull the soba noodles to my mouth
and hiss, un-making their long strings.
This is the sound of eating soba,
sucking in air, loud and energetic.
I hear wood rasp and tap
inside the bowls as they are drained
and clacked down on the counter empty.
Customers come and go through
the heat and steam of these small
kitchen shops, ordering soba,
soba o-kudasai!
I bow over your bowl
your body, your broth.
These are my hands that hold you.
This is the sound of my lips, warm
breathing you in
saying soba!

Home on the Range

We drank warm rice wine,
ate beef tongue and kimchi
and laughed deep from our bellies.

Someone handed me a microphone
and wanted me to sing
"Home on the Range."

I followed the words on a screen,
visions of prairies and fields.
Each time we walked through alleys

the room we went into got smaller
until it seemed we had stepped behind a wall.
I danced with the woman who sat on the bar.

At four in the morning I felt I'd known
my friend forever. With his head against
my arm, he said, I must go home.

We pissed in the streets and stopped a taxi.
He told the driver where to go.
I remember someone singing "Country Roads."

And I could swear I saw a man on the sidewalk
in his bathrobe with a golf club
practicing his swing.

In the English Teachers' Room

James tells us about
his correspondence classes
that will give him a degree

in hypnosis. His voice excited, dramatic,
he tries to hold our attention. Scott and Bill
sit in the smokers' corner, where nonsmokers

won't go. Staring over their coffee
and taking long drags, they look as if
they've just awoken in their suits and ties.

Then P.J. blusters in, pirouetting on his toes,
flapping his arms at his sides.
He complains his new Cardin suit

has been crushed on the train, says
he doesn't know why he even bothers
to look good. Alan spots me

from across the room, comes over
and says, *Hello David H.* With pale,
puffy face and slicked-back hair, he

seems to want to sell me something. He makes
a point of calling everyone by their name tags.
We all keep an eye on the huge, orange clock

that hangs above Amanda, who furiously shuffles
through shelves of student folders
that are supposed to be ordered alphabetically.

She wants to know who has taken Kimoko
or was she not put back where she should go.
Two minutes are left before it's time.

Everyone holds on to the blue books
we'll need to stay afloat.
I'm wondering again

about the power of suggestion.
Someone asks if "since"
is considered a preposition.

According to Tradition

This little arched bridge
is rebuilt every thirty years.
Carp, patron saints of children,
dart slowly in all directions.

Behind me, I hear the clear, polished
words, brought out for a special
occasion, *Good afternoon.*
When I turn around, I meet a man,
of my father's age, who tells me
he has lived in New Jersey
working for Sony, nearly thirty years,
and that sometimes in this country,
he feels like a stranger, too.

He brags about his daughter,
the fencing champion, who is expected
to come back every summer and stay
with her grandparents here, in Tokyo.
The next weekend I meet her.
She tells me, *they're a drag—*

I see her grandmother nag and jab
with her finger: she doesn't act Japanese.
Her grandfather shuffles through the house,
mumbling to himself. He pretends he cannot
hear his wife anymore. Everyday he goes out
to stand on the veranda to reach atop
the wooden fence that borders his yard,

where he keeps a row of bonzai.
With special tools he carefully pares
and props the old pines, transplanting them
from tray to tray, cutting the roots
that have grown too deep.

In Monsoon

Nothing to compare it to.
Neither East nor West.
From my bunk in the Bangkok boarding house,

I glimpse your belly, sandbar or shoal,
as you turn in your sleep. Later, we walk
along the river that circles the city,

past soot-stained windows, chickens
plucked and hung upside down, snake doctors'
charms and street vendors' food we won't eat.

City-scooters river up and down
the boulevard, the air thick with exhaust.
We will not talk about our pasts.

Under a room's slow-turning blades,
we navigate into night, like first
cartographers, charting hip and bone.

The next morning we ride a chuk-chuk
to the airport, garlands of flowers swinging
from on top metal sides painted bright colors

of mangoes and guavas sold in the streets.
I'm not going with you. What can we say?
We stepped outside our lives, a trick

we learned — like a woman
rising from a box, a man twisting
from chains. In Monsoon. Underwater.

Lying Under Branches

Cherry blossoms are falling,
and you will ride home
after work, drunk in a taxi.
Cherry blossoms are falling,
while children are carried
on their mothers' backs
or in front against breasts.
Cherry blossoms are falling.
You lean over another table
for the mamasan, pouring businessmen
drinks and lighting their cigarettes.
White and blowsy,
cherry blossoms are falling,
as hostesses in slippered feet
scurry around low tables,
their toes springy on matted floors.
The city is a sewer of blossoms.
Everyone drunk in the afternoon
lying under branches on soggy ground.
Romance, one hour in a love hotel,
something untold.
Cherry blossoms are falling.
Someone steps in front of a taxi
and is tossed in the air.

Sharif's Fish Stew

The smell of fish floats
under the crack of my door.
Sharif is cooking his weekly stew.
He carries the scent of his spices
in his hands and hair, and they
will not leave the soles of his feet,
though he washes them before prayer.
I believe his stew makes him strong.
Perhaps Muhammed can smell
the faith of his followers.

Sharif, my friend, keeps his faith
on the roof of our boarding house,
where he rents a tin shack that rattles
in the rain. He prays there at dawn
before riding the trains two hours
outside of the city to work in a factory.
He calls me King David and says I should try
some of his stew. It will give me strength,
the strength we must have at night for the women.
We laugh loud like sultans and kings.

I would like to write a few lines
that could last a week like Sharif's stew,
that would fill the air of kitchens,
because I have no prayers
and no recipe for my faith —
a few lines that could
linger in my palms
and not be washed away.

Anata

Riding the train I hold the loaf
of rye bread, still warm,
that I bought after work.
The crowds push
and I tuck it close,
soft in a paper bag.

Another time I meant to bring you
this bread, I put it above
where briefcases and hats
were supposed to go,
and letting my thoughts wander,
walked off at your station
feeling empty-handed.
I turned and saw it
cooling on the rack
just as the doors shut.

But today, all day, I confess
I thought of your body—
your hips in my hands,
your hair against my shoulder,
the sound of your voice calling me
with the familiar *anata*.

Konbawa,
you say like a bell,
as I slip out of my shoes,
come into your room,

bringing with me
the smell of a kitchen.
I set the loaf down
on the kotatsu table.

I love
what our hands say
when they feel
the warmth of our bodies,
how we'll break the bread
still fresh,
and hold each other
until morning.

Morning Ride on the Yamanote Line

The conductor's voice
glides over the drowsy heads,
like a familiar hand
smoothing unruly hair.
A schoolgirl in uniform
falls asleep on my shoulder
as the train tilts and sways.
She's forgotten about her satchel,
what she's carrying to school,
and sleeps in this brief lapse
of time before the day begins.
For a moment I have a sister, a child,
someone for whom I must be still.

The Willows of Ginza

The willows of Ginza
that ran along the Sumida river
are gone, cleared for wider roads,
replaced by the smaller ginkgo.
Between shorn, concrete banks,
I see a boat coming downstream
in evening, strung with lanterns,
shadows hopping in the yellow
light of paper screens, the rhythm
of drum and wail of samisen strings,
a low chant calling across the water.

Once I heard my mother weep.
I was standing in our yard,
holding a branch of willow —
its little buds would not
twist off easily in my hands —
when I heard her cry,
a sound I'd never heard before.
All was silent, as I listened
with oak, the buckeye, and maple.

I am there in the yard,
planted deep for my mother.
I have not gone anywhere.

II

The Prayer Wheel

The Kiss

This memory is like one of my father's slides. Only this is not a slide that my father could have taken, for he is in this picture. Indeed, he plays the leading man. We are standing in the kitchen, my mother, father, and I. I might be six or seven years old. I ask my parents to kiss. I've never seen them kiss before and don't know if they will really do it — kiss on command. Kiss for the show of it, for my own private viewing. Perhaps I've just seen two young adults my parents' age kiss in a movie, blown up on a big screen, or on T.V. in close-up. But I know enough to believe that when two people kiss it means they love each other.

I know the feeling of my mother's kisses at night and in the morning, or sometimes for no reason at all in the middle of the afternoon. I know the wet kiss from her finger that has just touched her tongue, a kiss to wipe away a smudge on the corner of my mouth or to pull back a stray hair from my eyes. I know the feeling of her lips on my forehead and cheeks, the kiss I must have every night before I go to sleep.

It is the middle of the afternoon, a Saturday or Sunday, light pouring into the kitchen. My father takes my mother in his arms and dips her. He presses his lips to hers, their arms wrapped tightly around each other. This is a real swoon of a kiss, an end-of-the-movie, heroic, leading-man and leading-woman kiss.

I begin to applaud and cheer. They hold each other in this pose for what seems like a long time, longer than I had expected, longer than I had wanted — as if, for a moment, they have forgotten about me, forgotten that I am standing here in the kitchen with them. Yet, as they kiss, I can imagine myself between them — even though their bodies are pressed together so tight.

Dust

The salesman who came to the door
smiled through the screen, his face
blurry in the afternoon light.
He was courteous. My mother let him in.
I'd been sitting in a chair for hours
watching dust swirl in sun motes.
I was five, a sphinx
guarding the silence of the house,
my mother and I alone in the afternoon.
He said he was selling a kind of
vacuum that filtered the air.
It sucked up dust we couldn't see.
Most dust he said is dry skin, flaked
and fallen off the body. We weren't aware
of how much we shed. He asked
how many lived in the house, said
we were breathing in our own
dead skin. My mother listened
and offered him some tea.
I wanted my father to be there.
The man smiled and knelt
on the living room floor to demonstrate
his machine, a box like the shell
of a turtle, an engine humming.
He poured out a cupful of air, measured
and weighed in dust. This, he said,
is what we were breathing.
He held up a small chalice, an urn
of all our family remains, as if it were

cremated ash, as if we could see
the germs, as if our family wasn't healthy
living in our house together, as if
we needed him to breathe.

Family Slide

In this family slide
my mother sits on a sandy beach
on a light blue and white beach towel,
her white sandals placed carefully
in front of her by the corner.
She is alone and leans against a breaker wall,
the grey-white concrete blending in with the sand.
She holds a book open on her lap,
no signs of any of us around:
no beach balls, Styrofoam surfboards, or inflatable rafts.
Just my mother sitting alone, holding
a new-looking paperback, the title
in big, bold, all-cap letters: "JENNIE."

The sun is bright and strikes the wall above her head,
like a tide-line of light. Her straw sun hat pushed back,
so the sunlight falls across her forehead and eyes.
She wears red lipstick and is squinting,
her legs crossed at the knees.
Her blue stretch pants stop just above her ankles.
Sand sticks to the soles of her feet.

This photograph of my mother is the one I love the most.
It gives me a chance to see her by herself—
a beautiful, solitary woman on a beach.
I am glad my father interrupted her reading that day,
and she looked up from the page,
smiling now for me to see.

Long Walk Home

Mother, I was late for your death.
But I know you have forgiven me.
You knew how easily I lost
track of time, hovering above a puddle.
That day I walked the half mile home
in two and a half hours, you were cross.
I threw away the stick that kept time
on trees and sidewalks, that led me astray
to poke and stir puddles,
where I divined long-legged striders
skating across the surface.

I can't say what I discovered that day,
what feather or stone I pulled
from the water. But I know
you would have listened, if I had told
its story. Just as now I want
to explain where I've been,
why I'm late to speak of you,
who are the story I'm telling.

The Patio

Al, whose dark eyes tapered at the corners,
would not finish a sentence;
his hands wiped away words.
When his red truck pulled into the driveway,
I helped him lug bricks and sand
around the house to the back.
Bent over, sweating by his side,
I leveled the ground, pressed down
in diagonal angles each colored brick:
bright auburn, terra cotta, rose.
I believed in what my hands could do.
When we finished Al warned if I didn't
moisten the sand, it would blow away.
That August I watered and swept the bricks,
waiting for my mother to get well,
to return to rest on the patio.

Tonight at dusk I walk along the Cuyahoga river,
trespass through woods, and come up to the house.
I am here in the fall of my twelfth year,
weeding the bricks, looking back
toward the yard that slopes to the woods
and the river I cannot see, slowly
carving a life line in the land.

The Circle

We always called it "the circle," my childhood street. One day my cousin Bill took my father, brother, and me up in a little three-passenger plane, and we flew over our neighborhood. I could see our street from the air, how it made a nearly perfect circle. The houses looked like little square boxes. And the driveways leading in looked like spokes.

From high up in the air, these homes were the size of the small plastic squares we moved around our Monopoly board, those green houses and red hotels. I could see which was my house, the little red ranch-style house at the furthest point from where Longmere Drive feeds into Marilyn, next to my neighbor Glenn Leppo's house with his backyard pool. I could see the river too, just beyond our back yard, how it twists and curves close to the circle, then flows beyond.

My mother didn't go up in the plane with us. Perhaps there wasn't room for her. It was just us boys adventuring in the sky, navigating through clouds, looking down at our neighborhood. My father took slides so that later he could project them on our basement wall for my mother to see.

A year later, when my mother died at two in the morning, my father, brother, and I came together in the living room with our arms around each other's shoulders, our heads bent down, like parachutists falling in a circle. We could not let go of each other.

Later that morning, my brother and I decided to go for a walk before the sun came up. We didn't want to stay in the house any longer. Outside the air was beginning to turn a light grey. Everything was perfectly still — the sky, the trees, the houses. We began walking around the circle. None of our neighbors had turned on their lights yet. We walked and talked, a little breathless, happy to be moving, swinging our arms, as if we needed to convince ourselves that we were still alive.

We passed our house every ten minutes or so, but didn't stop. We kept walking and talking. We agreed we both needed to help our father now, to be good to him. We talked as if we were making a pact with each other. Neither one of us could mention our mother or talk about ourselves, only about our father.

Our hearts pumped hard as we walked around and around the circle. We were glad to be doing something with our energy, to have some direction to go, which always brought us back again to the familiar front of our red house, our driveway spilling into the road. After awhile we began to repeat the same phrase, like a chant, our little mantra, *we need to help Dad, we need to help Dad.* And slowly the circle began to turn. From up above, it must have looked like a giant prayer wheel spinning — two boys walking along their street, the only thing moving at this hour of the morning.

The Prayer Wheel

Grandpa held the unicycle
while I balanced on one wheel.
I wanted to see how far I could go,
to learn something completely new
so when you returned, I could say, look at me!

I pushed off Dad's station wagon
and leaned as though I were falling,
but I was pedaling, bringing my legs
up from under, so my movement forward
caught me. There was no other way to go.

I practiced around parked cars,
Leppo's trash cans, and Bobby's
basketball hoop. Dressed in coat and tie,
I pedaled circles on our driveway,
the day we waited for your funeral.
My "no hands" were flags in the air,
waving a prayer, *look at me, mom,
look at me!*

Diana

Diana was your name, goddess
of the moon, goddess of the forest.
Now it is my invocation.

We search the heavens in pajama feet,
late summer nights on the driveway.
My brother leans over his telescope,
collecting data. I stand behind him,
distracted, moonstruck. I don't want
to take apart the moon, unwitch
its spell on me, spy on craters and seas.
We have maps to tell us where Orion
and the bear are supposed to be.
Look! he says. But I cannot reach.

At night everything stays on —
the stars, Venus, the moon,
your kiss on my cheek.
The sky blinks, Venus lays low.
The moon's powdered face seems
to know we're looking.

Leaving the House

It wouldn't be ours anymore,
my father explained. And I thought
I understood that day we carried
everything out — boxes of clothes,
kitchenware, lamps, books I'd never seen
boxed before. All day and then late
into the night, I helped my father.
We walked up the ramp into the dark
mouth of the van, until the cupboards
and closets were bare, all the rooms
opened like trick doors into nothing,
the house itself a big, empty box.

That night in September I kept
expecting to salvage something
I could carry in my arms.
As the air grew chill, my father
told me I was a good boy.

Years later, I won't remember
what we did with my mother's clothes.

Spaghetti Dinners

We move like strangers through the rooms,
dust rising up ladders of light.
My brother vacuums, until the cord tears
from the socket. I find cleanser
underneath the sink and lean over
the toilet, as I've seen my mother do,
amazed how easily dirt loosens, then swirls
down the drain. From the kitchen,
my father rattles the dishes, calls us in.
Wearing an apron, he stands above the stove,
stirring sauerkraut and wieners in a pan.
He calls it cooking.

Fridays we're glad to eat at Missimmi's.
We walk through the front door off Main Street
into the cool, dark dining room, as if
we are stepping into another country.
On the walls hang wicker bottles of wine,
glossy paintings of mountains and vineyards,
gondolas and Venetian canals.
My father sips his Chianti, while my brother and I
slurp sweet Cokes through a straw.
We always have the same waitress who
must be about my mother's age.
She wears a white dress and red apron
I never think is a uniform.
I order the usual, a plate of spaghetti
with a small sirloin steak on the side,

and she smiles. Later, she'll return
through the swinging kitchen doors
to circle our table, hovering warm plates
of spaghetti above our heads.
And for a moment, we will forget
there are only three of us
at the table.

Washing the Wok

This morning I wash the wok
then boil coffee with Guatemalan beans
I buy each week, weighed exactly on scales.
Outside the sun has evaporated
last night's bright puddles of neon.
Steam settles in cool beads on the window.

It's not enough to remember
how my mother left dinner early
and I followed her, how I held
a washcloth to cool her fever
and later washed the dishes, thinking
if only I could make them clean...
All summer she forgave me the peas
on my plate I would not finish.

I have counted the years, all the seasons
we ate together, against the hours
I scoured pots in the kitchen after she died.
Now I've learned to cook with woks,
to watch their drama as though they might
tell me something, and later to clean,
my hands in hot water —
I have not finished my grief.

III

Yellow Barn

Reading Virgil

In the kitchen this afternoon,
my father and I drink beer and grow
light-headed. He talks about the heavy feet
of Latin poetry, the story of
Aeneas: how he carried
his father from Troy with his little boy
and sad wife and, later, descended
into the shades; there, he tried three times
to hug his father, but couldn't.
I guess my father, like all sons,
is thinking about his own. *Romans,*
he concludes, *were solemn farts.*

Outside, the light is grey.
We feel the oven's heat, smell
tuna casserole wafting up.
He opens two more beers, his hands loose
and calm. He asks if I remember the day
I flew to Asia. He was in L.A.
at a conference reading a paper —
and drove away from the city.
He tells me he walked on the beach to watch
the planes rise above the water
and glint like gulls.
I didn't know when you'd be back,
he says, so close I could reach
across the table and touch him.

Red Kimono

Your postcard arrived today from Kyoto.
You write, *shibaraku desu ne,*
it's been a long time. You've gone back
to where maple leaves are painted
on sand-colored walls, there are seasons
for earthquakes, cherry blossoms and moon
viewing, festivals for children, harvest
and for remembering the dead.

You said you went to the temple market,
a clear, gorgeous morning,
bald men strolling about in robes, such cabinets,
kimonos and crockery — I would've liked it.
Do you remember the market in Komagome?
Still formal with each other, I held
the umbrella carefully between us
down an alley crowded with vegetables
and fresh fish; rain dripped from awnings
as we walked on the ocean's floor, you reciting
the names for all that bounty,
strange talismans on your tongue.

Rather than talk about your father's cancer,
you told me what he loved — collecting
magazines, old bikes, shoe boxes
of odd parts — and recalled
you could not squeeze through the garage,
overloaded with flea market trinkets.
He collected languages too — his gift for tongues
he gave you, so many ways to name.

We carry our affections far —
translating from bone to breath,
we thread them back into this world.
I remember the red kimono you sewed
with scraps from a silk factory, printed
designs of plum blossoms and cranes,
whatever falls or flies away. One night,
standing in my doorway, unlike the Japanese,
you didn't hide your smile. We stepped out
into the glow of shoji lanterns, gauzy
neon light, past vendors selling octopus
and squid, huge radishes and beans.
You named everything I pointed to,
but I needed nothing, as we walked side
by side. You wore your bright kimono,
swinging your wide, airy sleeves.

My Mother's Body

What did I know about my mother's body? I knew she liked to take baths. I used to look at the sides of the tub just after she had bathed. I'd see a foamy, grey film of suds stuck to the walls with bits of skin and hair. Sometimes I saw my mother leaning over the tub, scrubbing the sides with Comet, until the chalky water swirled down the drain. Once, I opened the bathroom door accidentally and saw her naked. I don't remember this scene very well, only the image of her breasts just above the water. Her hair, though, is a memory I have been able to treasure. I used to bury my face in my mother's thick, black hair and search for the eyes she said were in the back of her head. How else could she always know what I was doing? Our game gave me an excuse to dig, part those dark strands to see her dry, white scalp. Perhaps I wanted to be scared, see something ugly underneath such beauty. I think of the hairbrush my mother left on her dresser and this haiku by Buson: *Sudden chill / dead wife's comb in our bedroom / I step on.* I used to inspect my mother's hair wrapped tightly around the bristles. I often watched her as she picked at the brush, untangling her long strands. For years after she died, the memory of my mother's hair grew in my mind, a forest from which I could not escape. I was attracted to women who had hair like hers. When I embraced a girl, I often thought about my mother. I loved her as any twelve-year-old boy may love his mother, his first love — her smile, her eyes, her soft hands. Only my mother died, and I still cannot pull my face from that dark thicket.

Why We Dream

for my brother

Because you won't come home, I fly
to the Rockies to see you. Driving away
from the airport, you clench your jaw,

tell me you don't know what to do
with your life. A solar physicist,
you claim you don't do science anymore.

Always flying to another meeting,
you're never in one place long.
You don't know why but sometimes

you cry in airports. Remember how you
questioned the world, peering at planets
and cells? You swapped Asimov novels

with Dad. You entered the contest,
"Tell Me Why," sponsored by
Lou Lyman Chevrolet, and asked

the winning question: why do we dream?
At his dealership, Lou's voice boomed
from his barrel-chest. He shook your hand

awarding the prize: a complete set
of New Book of Knowledge Encyclopedias.
We read the answer in volume D:

We dream because we must, each night
jumbling notes on the blackboard.
We thumbed pages, believing the world

was alphabetized. On the cover were two
tear-shaped halves of the globe, like the maps
inside airline magazines, fractured continents

sewn together with red flight routes.
As we drive these mountain roads,
I want to tell you this: Once I dreamed

about our mother in her hospital room.
All the beds were in shadow.
I'd returned from far away

to bring her home. She whispered
her Texas accent soft in my ear.
Only her tone I remember, no words.

The last time I saw Lou Lyman,
you'd been gone for years. I walked
down rows of shiny new and used cars.

Lou was old, his left eye half-closed.
His voice, shaky, as though he couldn't make
a pitch, as though in the end, he knew

all his dream cars were lemons.
Driving now in your old Honda,
you won't trade in, we see jagged peaks,

far from the flat world we grew up in.
For your work you need to be
this close to the sky. You tell me

these mountains are young, still growing.
I want to tell you
we'll spend our lives dreaming

of returning to a place
that's only a tone of voice.

Passim's Cafe

Like early photographs of motion,
light flashed through windowframes
that lined the wall. In the basement
where I worked, I watched legs lift and fall
against grey sidewalk and discovered
the sheer effort of walking,
how bodies leaned against some force.
Each day the same man passed the windows,
knees punching at his overcoat; he was
the first to appear in the doorway.
With an air of exhaustion, he'd unpeel
his thick tweed. No one knew anything about him
but that he taught at Harvard and ordered
liverwurst on rye with lettuce; always, he ate
slowly, picking his chips one by one.

When I was late, he was there, standing
below street level on the stairs, bashful
and anxious to be let in. I think
it was not the cold drizzle so much
as people that he wanted to escape.
Eventually he didn't have to order.
I'd fetch a few heads of lettuce
from the cooler, slam one to the counter,
so the core crumbled and the leaves
fanned and pulled apart easily;
then measure and dole the soft, pink
liverwurst evenly across the rye.
Once when I asked how things were going,
he put his hands on the table and smiled:

Well, I'm not complaining. At a certain point
in life, you realize happiness
is just a matter of avoiding pain.

I was young, I pitied him for his habits
and fears, his flimsy little liverwurst
sandwich I was sick of making.
That winter my radiator sputtered
without steam; I slept in my clothes and stumbled
to un-thaw each morning against the stove.
I heard children's voices float up
from down the street, wild, half-human
shrieks. Like a fish-eye lens, I roamed
the city, focusing on others, half-frozen,
pushing shopping cart loads of recyclable cans.

Each day I was glad to descend
into steamy smells of chili and soup,
where kettles boiled over, and parsley stems
and carrot skins fell across the floor.
I dipped my hands into the heat of the oven
to pull sheets of brownies from the rack,
sweets the liverwurst man never tasted.
While others hummed with talk and gesture,
he sat calmly, one bite left, a frill
of lettuce hanging limp.

He'd stare as if I had disappeared
in the copper light of afternoon.
I wiped off tables and pushed in chairs.

The sun broke in shafts across the floor;
legs flickered and reeled in the windows.
I thought happiness was a kind of motion.
I galloped through light, dreaming
what I'd do with my life,
how I'd walk up these stairs, quit
this city, and shake the ashes from my hair.

Lambis Reads My Palm

Lambis takes my hand; his long fingers
that draw the music from the keys
are surprisingly square.

He turns my palms toward candlelight,
holds them in custody; I await the verdict.
Bravo! he says. Everyone crowds to gaze

at the star in my palm, promising luck
and creativity. His fingernail drags
a narrow groove, like a stylus lifting music

from a record, then leaps to a parallel line.
Friends, Lambis tells me I have many
and congratulates me for my good fortune.

Poets and musicians, he says, *make great friends.*
Lambis can't understand why in this country
universities buy Nautilus before new pianos.

The old Cadillac he purchased at night
from an Iranian in Toledo cost him
a thousand dollars to repair;

the doors stick, the windows won't open.
*When I return to Greece, I'll say to my friends
I drove a Cadillac in America.*

Already he has a contract to record,
his life running a course, sure
as the Brahms he played this evening.

Truth or silence! he warns.
In my country, we sing our poetry.
That's how we know it's good.

Two Dumas

My father calls in mid-November,
wakes me up to say he's rhymed

intent with sentiment.
And would I like to hear it?

I'm sure he's been up since four,
the house dark around him.

He prefers the nineteenth century
and dreams we're famous writers,

like Dumas *père* and Dumas *fils*.
Last time I saw him,

he didn't want to hear my poem,
but said he'd rather read it.

Now I listen; though, he warns,
it's better on the page.

Reaching to a Sky of Soba

I walk past winter boots lined up in rows,
through the door: Ms. Brown's ten o'clock 5-A English.
My first day teaching poetry in the schools
the students crowd around.
They want to know how tall I am
and if my hair is real.
A stranger in their room, I stand near
a small stool they call the author's chair.
Snow falls outside, beyond
windows dressed with pilgrim hats and turkeys.
Reading my poem, "Eating Soba,"
I say poetry lets you talk to things
you don't normally talk to, and
here, I'm talking to noodles,
as though my bowl were a smiling friend.
In Japan, you can slurp as loud
as you want. The louder,
the greater the compliment to the chef.
The class practices slurping.
One boy asks,
Could you say the sky is a bowl of soba?
I smile, yes!
Then the sun is a raw egg floating in it!
Another hand appears.
Trees are chopsticks.
Heads turn to look out the windows.
And clouds are steam rising above.
The students gasp and applaud.
Planets are onions.

The moon is a bump at the bottom of the bowl.
Earthquakes break up the noodles, their rumbling is slurping.
Our mouths are Black Holes breathing it in.
God is the chef.
Meteors are coins we throw down to pay.
Then the shy boy, looking at the floor, raises his hand.
The universe is a giant bowl of soba.
We keep eating and eating until the last explosion.
When the universe ends, he says, *our bowl is empty.*
The bell rings, their hands still reaching in the air.

My Father in the Stacks

For hours in his study he'd disappear
into the private chambers of a story.
Walls within walls, his bookshelves
dwarfed me. His large oak desk
held the family photo, tall, straight stacks,
and the yellow plots of legal pads.
Sometimes he'd pass me a book
if my hands were clean.

I've grown tall like my father
wandering dark hours of the afternoon
in fields of print, rustling pages.
Back home at the university
where my father teaches, I walk
through the library on the seventh
floor, no call number in mind.
I turn the aisle and he is there.
In the silence of so many books,
we do not know what to say.
I forgive our unwritten lives,
the years we haven't read.
We pass each other, my hands are clean.

Driving Pauline to the Airport

Driving Pauline to the airport
does not have to be a poem about much.
This morning I had a bowl of café au lait
after sleeping alone because I'm sick,
a small cold but nothing serious.
Lunch at the diner with Sarah.
We ate treasure bran muffins
cream cheese custard filling.
She gave me the last of hers.
I think I'm in love
with the way things happen,
our schedules today,
grey skies, grey sweater,
her arm around my waist
as we stepped out of the diner.
I could never be done
with this life,
doing friends favors,
driving Pauline to the airport.

I took off my watch today
because each second ticked
so noticeably.
What a wonderful thing
all this time,
and the words we have to describe it.

Drew told me this morning
most viruses are passed
through the eyes, and I thought
he meant by just looking.

But it's when your finger
touches someone sick,
then touches your eye.

Mary called me a diehard
as she poured me more tea.
She knows how to waitress with the best of them
and pivots on her toes,
caught in cross-fires of orders and needs.
So this is a poem for Mary, too,
who offers over-the-counter hugs,
mothers us with honey and lemon,
impatient with customers who can't decide.

I can't decide what I love more,
to watch or hear
Sarah play the violin.
When I return
she'll be rehearsing with Drew,
fingers dancing furiously.

I'll tell her about
driving Pauline to the airport,
what I'm thankful for,
her music,
the way she frowns when she plays,
so serious, like today,
she locked her fingers in mine,
as we sat on swivel seats
in a railroad car that stopped
one day in town and never left.

Yellow Barn

We do not say what we'll have to sink
into the barn that looms large, painted yellow
against the sky, the name Brigham
still legible on the old slate roof. Yet now
the hayloft, silo, and milking stalls
stand empty, more like a stage set
than a working barn.

Today our ragtag crew labored on the old front doors.
We tore down rusted track, scaled ladders side by side,
and heaved up new twelve-foot sections.
We drilled lag bolts deep into chestnut beams.
By day's end, we hung the doors: *Dead plumb!*
and shimmed the bottoms snug against the floor.
Wheels packed in well-oiled ball-bearings
rolled inside the track, while a bat crawled from a slit,
unfolding its origami wings. Doors slid open,
a heavy rumble above our heads, like the sound
of a train passing through fields at night.

All day James worried about the oval
oak table he found buried in the barn
beneath a tarp covered with bats' black dung—
where to position it for dinner
so we cannot see the silo's roof caved in, rotted
window frames tilted into parallelograms,
warped siding, bowed out, the whole barn
sagging like a sunken ship that will take years to salvage.

Outside, in wavering candlelight,
we sit down to flowers, blue linen,

and Pauline's garden: pesto, summer squash,
ratatouille, cucumbers and dill, chicken
basted in basil and garlic. For years now
I have sat at these make-shift dinner tables
with this family I have adopted as my own.
Pauline cannot pass a dish without
advice or warning: this corn
should be the sweetest, or she muses
why this year's tomatoes ripened small.
We praise her food. Then Matthew,
her son, brings coffee and
his Norton anthology from the house.
Pauline unwraps raspberry cobbler.
Clockwise, she sends the steaming bowls,
while Matthew rattles onionskin pages.
He cups a candle to read from Whitman
and smiles toward his father:
The big doors of the country barn
stand open and ready, the dried grass
of the harvest-time loads the slow-drawn wagon.
I am there, I help, I came stretch'd atop of the load...

James shrieks, amused at his son's selection.
It's exactly that poem that got him
started on this crazy barn business.
Now that's ironic, Pauline says,
this dreamy man in charge. Her finger
plants a seed in his arm and repeatedly
all her worries come back: that the only
bounty the barn will store is bats.

We've all grown uncommonly quiet
as this late summer night stalls.
Our lantern faces glow around the table.
Soon we'll leave each other and return
to September's classrooms, hard floors,
like land after months at sea.
Yet tonight, gathering dishes,
beginning to drift toward the house,
I can see the barn whole, large
as a cathedral, the cows in their stalls,
the hay loft filled with hay,
almanacs, seed calendars, and milking charts
hanging on the walls like scripture.

Household Gods

for Lynn

Funny how happiness doesn't need
words, but is more like humming,
a purr in the back of the throat.
When we're lucky, it declares us
home, climbing through a window,
following our steps from room to room,
like the cat that found you sitting
on the porch. It must have known where to go.
We were careful in naming him, knowing
he's been called by other names.

I feel lucky with you, as though
happiness could find us anywhere.
Driving today, we looked for
lawn ornaments and saw a giant Buddha.
We stepped around a pink flamingo, pudgy
cherubs, a figure of Jesus praying,
until we found, smiling back at us,
a statue of a woman carrying two baskets.
She was chipped with one arm half-broken.
We got her for a steal and placed her
in the garden, where we feel at home
on our knees, pulling weeds, pinching
aphids, praying against leaf wilt
and vine borer. Barefoot, she stands
between the mint and basil, repeating
the steady hum of green.

Acknowledgments

Grateful acknowledgment is made to the editors of the following journals in which some of these poems (or earlier versions of them) first appeared:

Akron Life & Leisure: "My Father in the Stacks"

Anathema Review: "Lambis Reads My Palm"

Artful Dodge: "My Mother's Hair;" "The Kiss"

Behind Bars: "Leaving the House"

English Journal: "Dust;" "Household Gods;" "Driving Pauline to the Airport;" "Passim's Cafe;" "Two Dumas"

5AM: "Eating Soba;" "The Patio;" "Reading Virgil"

Indiana Review: "Red Kimono," previously entitled "Travel Can Be a Way of Mourning"

Ohio Teachers Write: "Yellow Barn"

Paper Street: "In Monsoon," previously entitled "In Bangkok"

Tar River Poetry: "Long Walk Home;" "The Prayer Wheel"

The Sun: "The Circle"

Whiskey Island Magazine: "Reaching to a Sky of Soba"

"My Father in the Stacks" is anthologized in *What Have You Lost* (Greenwillow Books, 1999)

"O-bon" is anthologized in *This Time, This Place* (The Poets' League of Greater Cleveland, 1996).

"Red Kimono," previously entitled "Travel Can Be a Way of Mourning," is anthologized in *Writing Our Lives: Laughter, Loss, and Love* (The Poets' League of Greater Cleveland and The National Association for Poetry Therapy, 1997).

"Reaching to a Sky of Soba" is anthologized in *Learning By Heart: Contemporary American Poetry about School* (University of Iowa Press, 1998).

"Family Slide" and "Leaving the House" are anthologized in *Family Matters: Poems of our Families* (Bottom Dog Press, 2005).

Some of these poems originally appeared in the chapbook, *Sabishi: Poems from Japan,* which won The Wick Chapbook Series Contest (Kent State University Press).

"Red Kimono," previously entitled "Travel Can Be a Way of Mourning," won an Associated Writing Programs Intro Journal Award.

My thanks to my friend, David Prittie, for his artwork and original design of this book and for the vision of my publisher, Tony Gorsline. I am grateful to the Ohio Arts Council, Ragdale Foundation, and Vermont Studio Center for fellowships which assisted me in writing these poems.

A special thanks to my wife, Lynn, and to my many friends who have helped with criticism of individual poems as well as the structure of this collection.

About the Publishers

Bedbug Press was founded in 1995 by Tony Gorsline, who has had a life-long love of books and writing. His inaugural publishing effort was *Going Over the Falls,* a collection of poetry, by Gretchen Sousa.

The name Cloudbank Books was established in 2000 by Peter Sears and Michael Malan with the publication of *Millennial Spring — Eight New Oregon Poets.*

Cloudbank Books became an imprint of Bedbug Press in 2002. Since that time, Bedbug Press has established, under its Cloudbank imprint, the Northwest Poetry Series and The Rhea and Seymour Gorsline Poetry Competition. In 2005, *Woman in the Water: A Memoir of Growing Up in Hollywood,* by Dorinda Clifton, was published by Bedbug Press. *Woman in the Water* is a creative non-fiction memoir. It is our hope that all of the Bedbug / Cloudbank books express our commitment to quality in writing and publishing.